The Birth
of Krishna

First published in 2008 by
Franklin Watts
338 Euston Road
London
NW1 3BH

Franklin Watts Australia
Level 17/207 Kent Street
Sydney
NSW 2000

A CIP catalogue record for this book is available
from the British Library.

ISBN 978 0 7496 8368 9 (hbk)
ISBN 978 0 7496 8374 0 (pbk)

Series Editor: Melanie Palmer
Series Advisor: Dr Barrie Wade
Series Designer: Peter Scoulding

Printed in China

Franklin Watts is a division of
Hachette Children's Books,
an Hachette Livre UK company
www.hachettelivre.co.uk

HOPSCOTCH
STORIES OF
RELIGION

The Birth of Krishna

by Anita Ganeri and Barbara Vagnozzi

W
FRANKLIN WATTS
LONDON•SYDNEY

About this book

The story of the birth of Krishna comes from the religion of Hinduism. Hinduism began at least 4,500 years ago in north-west India. Stories play an important part in Hinduism. They help to teach people about their faith in a way that is easy to understand. From an early age, Hindu children read and listen to stories about the gods and goddesses, and about events in the Hindu year. *The Birth of Krishna* introduces us to Krishna, one of the best loved Hindu gods. He is often shown with dark blue skin, the colour of a dark rain cloud.

Long ago, in India, there lived
a wicked king. His name was
King Kamsa.

King Kamsa had a beautiful sister called Devaki. She was sweet and kind to everyone.

She married a handsome prince,
called Vasudeva, who came to live
at the court.

One day, a wise man came to see King Kamsa with a terrible warning.

"Be careful, your Majesty,"
he said. "Your sister's eighth
child will kill you."

King Kamsa was furious. He
marched around the palace,
ranting and raving.

He threw Devaki and Vasudeva
in prison. They were guarded day
and night.

As the years went by, Devaki and
Vasudeva had seven babies.
All of them were girls.

The wicked king took each baby away as soon as it was born and killed it.

One night, Devaki gave birth to her eighth child. He was a beautiful baby boy.

She called the baby Krishna. She could not bear to hand him over to the evil king.

"Quickly! Let me take him away," said Vasudeva, "I will make sure that he is safe."

Vasudeva took the baby and crept out of prison. The gods helped to hide him as he crept past the guards.

He ran down to the river, lifted
Krishna above his head and
waded across to the other side.

Then he made his way to the
nearest house. A cowherd and
his wife lived there.

Vasudeva took the cowherd's baby
girl from her cradle and laid
Krishna there instead.

Then he took the little girl and
hurried back to the prison to tell
Devaki that their son was safe.

Next day, King Kamsa came
looking for the baby. Devaki
handed over the little girl.

When the king tried to kill her, the baby flew away. She was really a goddess!

King Kamsa was very angry at being tricked. "I'll find your baby," he promised.

But Krishna was safe in the
cowherd's village. He was loved
and well cared for.

Many years later, a messenger told
the king that Devaki's eighth child,
called Krishna, was still alive.

So the cunning king invited
Krishna to a wrestling match and
set two mighty giants against him.

But the king's evil plan failed.
First, Krishna killed the giants
stone dead.

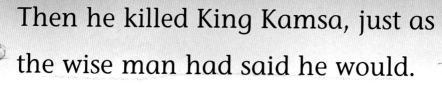

Then he killed King Kamsa, just as
the wise man had said he would.

Krishna was really the god, Vishnu.
Gods use disguises to appear
on Earth.

Every year, in late summer, people celebrate Krishna's birthday and how good won over evil.

Hopscotch has been specially designed to fit the requirements of the Literacy Framework. It offers real books by top authors and illustrators for children developing their reading skills.

For more details go to:
www.franklinwatts.co.uk

* hardback